LEARN HOW TO
FLY FISH IN ONE DAY

LEARN HOW TO
FLY FISH
IN ONE DAY

Quickest Way to Start Tying Flies, Casting Flies, and Catching Fish

Sylvester Nemes

Stackpole Books

Published by
STACKPOLE BOOKS
Cameron and Kelker Streets
P.O. Box 1831
Harrisburg, PA 17105

Printed in the U.S.A.

Library of Congress Cataloging-in-Publication Data

Nemes, Sylvester.
    Learn how to fly fish in one day.

    1. Fly fishing. I. Title.
SH456.N44 1986   799.1'2   85-20802
ISBN 0-8117-2185-X

Contents

A Word from the Author

So you want to learn how to fly fish. Thousands of men and youngsters (and more and more women) are learning how every year. They're enjoying this clean, gentile, and pristine sport that causes little or no damage to nature and — because of today's prevalent catch-and-release philosophy — little or no damage to trout and other fish.

Another good way besides this book to learn how to fly fish is to attend one of the fine schools that have developed. If you have the means and the time, fly-fishing school could be your best way. Or you might ask a fly-fishing friend for help. But don't be thwarted by possible negative responses. Here are some of the comments you might get:

"It'll take you years to learn how to cast."

"It's something you're either born with or you're not."

"You'll need a degree in entomology."

Such behavior shows fly-fishing snobbism. If you like, you can practice it, too, after you learn the sport.

The truth is that, with or without an angling friend, you can learn how to fly fish in one day. You won't be ready to win casting tournaments, and your form may give you away. But from this little book, you can become proficient and knowledgeable enough to catch a trout or other fish on your first outing.

The book is based on the 8-hour day:

Three hours to learn how to cast.

Three hours to learn how to fish (not including the time it might take to get to the river or lake).

And one hour each on learning how to tie flies and knots.

You could spend more time or less in any category, depending on what might interest you most. And there's no law against doing just a little each day through a period of several days.

I suggest you study the photos carefully and read the book through before starting any of the lessons. That way, you can get a feel for the sport before you actually start casting.

I want to thank Bob Heine and Janet Stoy, who posed for many of the photos, and my son Eric, who shot the photography. — S.N.

1

Equipment

It doesn't seem possible that a fly rod (never say pole) could get any stronger, lighter, or more beautiful and easy to cast with than today's rod made of graphite. With an 8-foot or 8½-foot rod of this material, you should be able to start from scratch and cast 30 or 40 feet in a very short time.

Fly lines, too, are marvels of technology. They require virtually no care (as they did when I started fishing). And their sizes (thickness and weight) are expressed simply in numbers (the smaller the number, the lighter the weight). Lines start at number 3 and go all the way to number 12, the heaviest and longest. The average line is right around a 6, and I recommend that size for beginners.

Your third piece of equipment is the fly reel. In fly

fishing, the fly reel is of relatively low importance because it is basically a storage and winching machine. (You pull line off the reel with your hand to prepare for casting, and you fight larger fish by turning the handle and retrieving the line at a speed regulated by the fish.)

Rod, line, and reel: Those are your three basic components for fly fishing. At the time I'm writing this book, you can get all three components, matched and ready to go, for anywhere from $50 to $100. If you settle for a rod made of glass fibers instead of graphite (the modern order of development is bamboo, glass, and graphite) you could spend a little less. But you could also spend a lot more for a rod made of either glass or graphite.

Attached to the end of your fly line is the leader. Its purpose is to connect the relatively heavy and thick fly line to the nearly weightless fly. Another purpose of the leader is to disguise from the fish the fact that you're indirectly connected to the fly.

Leaders are generally tapered. The heavier end is knotted to the line, and the lighter end is knotted to the fly (knots are coming in a later chapter). Leaders are made from nylon monofilament and come in various lengths, the average being 9 feet. You can buy leaders ready-made or make them yourself by tying together monofilament sections of varying diameters.

With a rod, line, reel, leader, and flies, you could go fly fishing without buying one single other thing. That's the way to start out.

But, eventually, if you want to walk in the water and keep your feet and legs dry and warm, you'll need waders. Before deciding which type to invest in, give the question much thought. Many fly-fishing people also wear a vest. You may decide to do likewise before long. A fly-fishing vest has many pockets, which you can fill with fly boxes, fluids to help your fly float, fluids to help your fly sink, spools of monofilament for making leaders, tippet material (each time you change flies or lose one in a fish's mouth or tree, you lose a bit of the leader's tippet). To maintain the leader's original length, you tie on new tippet material.

Knife. Thermometer. Scale. Repellent. Vests are also great for hanging or pinning things on. Landing nets. Spring-loaded retriever to hold a pair of clippers. Spring-loaded retriever with ruler. Wading staff and shooting basket. All thoughts for the future. But now, the basics.

Buying your first fly-fishing outfit is relatively simple today. Perhaps 500 fishing-tackle dealers across the land specialize in fly fishing. They're listed in the Yellow Pages, usually under "Fishing Tackle Dealers." Any one of them worthy of the name will be happy to help you put together an efficient combination of the three basic components. Very often they will have "starter specials" of rod, reel, and line all assembled and ready to go.

2

Casting: 3 Hours

Your 8-foot or 8½-foot fly rod (suitable for use with a 6-weight line) is probably in two sections. First make sure you align the guides on the tip section with those on the butt section. Then join the sections. Now get ready to attach the fly reel (notice that it hangs down). If you're right-handed, the reel handle goes on the left side of the rod. Your right hand will hold the rod. If you are left-handed, just reverse all the instructions I give for righties.

Oldtimers like myself have the reel handle on the right side and switch the rod to the left hand when we get a fish on, so that we can wind the fish in with our "natural" right hand. Right-handed beginners, however, will be miles ahead by learning to cast and play a fish with the right hand and crank the reel with the

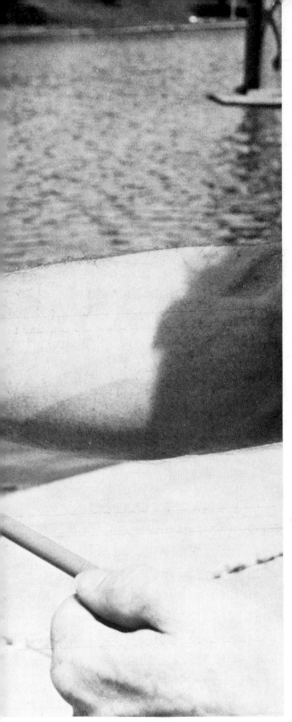

Before you join the two sections of your fly rod, make certain that the guides are properly aligned.

left, thus eliminating the need to transfer the rod from hand to hand.

Let's say your outfit is properly assembled (instructions on the details are coming up soon). You have the rod sections aligned and the reel properly attached.

Now pull five or six feet of line off the reel. The leader should already be attached (check the chapter on knots). Throw your hat down onto the ground and stick the rod butt and the reel into it. Hold the end of the *line* (not the leader) in your hand, and rest the rod at an angle in your other hand.

Incidentally, don't bother to set the hat down carefully. That won't do. Throw it down disdainfully, making sure it lands open-side up. Famous Western guides do this beautifully, going through perhaps three or four hats every fishing season. The idea is to keep your reel clean and protect it from sand and rocks.

Now you have the end of the line in your hand and are ready to string the line up through the guides. Fold the line over between thumb and forefinger, and run the loop through every guide. (It's a lot easier to thread the heavy line loop than it is to thread the thin leader.) When you get through the tip-top guide, pull the line and leader through until both are hanging freely. Now tie to the end of the leader a small piece of bright-colored cloth or yarn, which will substitute for the fly. (Notice that you've already spent 8 or 10 minutes doing these things and haven't even started to cast yet.)

To prepare for stringing line through rod guides, throw your hat onto the ground and place rod handle and reel in it.

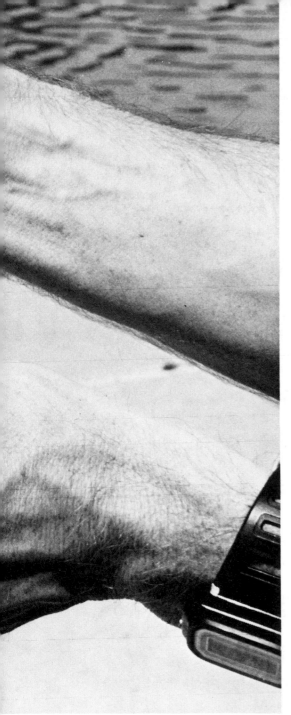

Easiest way to thread line and attached leader through rod guides is by making a loop in line and handling it as shown.

Best place to learn how to cast is on a hard, dry surface such as a concrete or asphalt driveway. You could also use a nice, wide lawn, preferably one with the grass cut close. You will need another person to help with the first couple of steps, although you could learn solo by skipping the first few steps.

With your helper standing by, pull 20 or 25 feet of line off the reel. Hand the end to your helper and ask him or her to carry it behind you. (NOTE: For greater visibility in the photos, we have used a large-diameter cotton cord in place of a standard fly line.)

Now raise the rod, forming a right angle at your elbow. Hold the rod handle comfortably, with only your thumb on the top side. Ask your helper to pull the line back, holding it as high as possible, developing a bend in the rod. If your helper is shorter than you, he or she could stand on something strong to even the line. Flex the rod forward several times. You will feel the spring and power built into the rod.

Next, ask your partner to take a position the same distance in front of you with the line and do the same thing. Your partner should hold the line high. Now you're flexing the rod in the opposite direction, backwards. Flex the rod back several times to feel the action.

The backward and forward bending of the rod and the power these motions apply give you about the same feelings (but to a much lesser degree) that you'll get later on when you're casting properly. Notice that the line, leader, and fly will travel as far in one direction as your partner has held it in the other.

Great. Now ask your helper to return to the first position behind you and hold the line high, ready to release it at the count of three. Flex the rod forward again, and count out loud to three. On three, push the rod forward smartly. Push forward as if you were using a hammer, trying not to "break" your wrist. If your partner has counted with you and released the line on "three," it will travel quickly through the air and extend itself in front of you approximately the same distance. You have made your first forward cast. Congratulations. Do several of these casts to get the feel of the line traveling forward.

Now ask your partner to go in front of you, carrying the line (or you can simply turn yourself around). You're ready for the back cast. Your partner again will hold the line high, this time in front of you. At the count of three, your partner releases the line and you throw it backward over your shoulder. Keep your wrist rigid, without breaking. Do both the forward and backward casts with your partner several times. Your synchronization will get better and better, and you'll find you can increase the length of the line slightly in both directions.

You won't need your partner for the rest of the instruction.

Take 20 to 25 feet of line to a position behind you, where your helper stood previously, and lay the line down on the grass or pavement. Straighten the leader out as far as it will go, and return to the rod.

While your helper holds end of line aloft behind you, flex the rod forward and put a bend in it about like this.

At the count of three, push the rod forward smartly as if you were driving a nail with a hammer, not bending your wrist.

To learn back cast, have your partner hold line aloft in front of you. After you flex rod several times, have partner release line at count of three.

For the unassisted forward cast, start with line and leader stretched out behind you, raise rod, and push it forward smartly.

Raise the rod as you did when your partner was helping. Then push the rod smartly forward to make your first unassisted forward cast. Try not to break the wrist. The line, leader, and "fly" will travel through the air about the same distance in front of you as it was stretched out behind you.

Do this maneuver several times, trying to lengthen the cast and adjust the power required to lift the line off the grass or driveway. (The smooth surface of concrete or asphalt offers less friction than grass, allowing a cleaner pickup of line and leader.)

Reverse the procedure. Carry the line, leader, and "fly" to a position 20 to 25 feet in front of you. Again, straighten out the leader and walk back to the rod. Hold the rod and point it toward the line at about a 45° angle. Bring the rod up smartly, aiming to throw the line behind you as far and as high as possible. Keep your hand and wrist locked as one unit when you bend your elbow. The line should travel as far behind you as it was extended in front of you. Practice the back cast several times until you recognize the motion and power necessary to lift the line and throw it backward.

So far, you've been casting with a fixed length of line and only one hand. The left hand up until now (assuming you're a right-handed person) has done nothing. Now, you begin to learn how to use your left hand as you'll use it when you're actually casting in a river or lake.

Stretch the line out behind you again, and return

to the rod. Hold the line in your left hand, and repeat the forward cast. Then stretch the line in front of you, holding the line in your left hand. Repeat the back cast. Do both casts several times. Notice how the line wants to slide out through the guides when the rod moves backward or forward.

You're ready now to fly cast as you will in actual fishing. You won't have a partner hold the line, and you won't carry it ahead of or behind you.

Pull 12 or 15 feet of line off the reel. While holding the rod in your right hand and the line in your left, shake the rod tip from side to side. Watch the rod tip while you're doing this. You'll see the line move through the tip top. Hold the rod handle higher than the tip to make the line go out faster.

When you have worked 15 or 20 feet of line out like this, bring the rod backward sharply, just as you did in the back cast with your partner and with the line stretched out in front of you. Stop the rod's backward motion directly over your right shoulder, just about aligned with your ear. Pause and take a short breath. Then push the rod forward to about the starting angle. Keep your wrist locked. You just made your first real cast. Congratulations.

Stopping the rod in mid-air on the back cast helps keep the line high in the air behind you. Then the pause permits the line to straighten out behind you. *The mid-air stop and the brief pause are probably the two most important points in fly casting.*

If your helper is still available, have him or her

For unassisted back cast, stretch line out ahead of you, bring rod to 45° angle, and then use rod to throw line behind you.

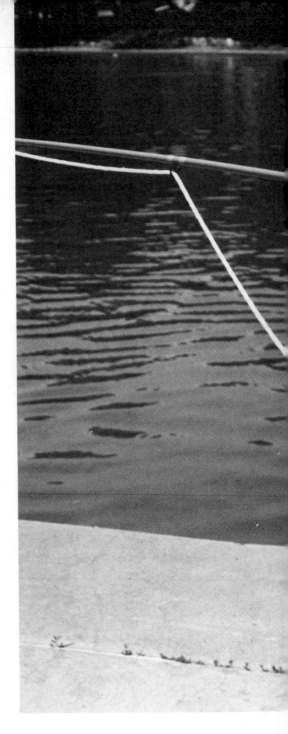

Left hand of righthander pulls line from reel when it's needed and strips in line on retrieve. (White yarn replaces fly line here for better visibility in photos.)

By holding the rod at this angle and shaking the rod tip from side to side, you make line move out through the tip top.

Notice this position carefully. As you get the hang of things, this is about as far back as rod should go on back cast.

After pausing to allow line and leader to straighten out behind you, use the nail-driving motion to make forward cast.

observe your back cast to make sure you're stopping the rod and keeping the line high. Practice these casts until you become familiar with the timing. You can observe the timing of the back cast yourself by turning your body to your right and lifting your head while you're casting.

Your next step is to connect your back cast and your forward cast, over and over again without letting the line fall. This maneuver is called false casting. You'll understand the usefulness of false casting when you want to add distance to your casting or when you fish a dry fly. In false casting, you pause on the back cast to let the line straighten out behind you, and then you pause on the forward cast to let the line straighten out in front of you.

Start out with 18 or 20 feet of line. Then add line by pulling it off the reel without stopping your false casting. You will notice something: As the line gets longer, you must pause longer.

All of your casting practice so far has begun to prepare you for fishing areas where you have unlimited room behind you. In actual fishing, though, you'll find yourself in areas where trees, bushes, or high banks limit or even prevent a back cast. In these situations, you can use the roll cast. It's really quite simple.

Start by stretching 18 or 20 feet of line in front of you on the lawn or pavement. Hold the rod in your right hand, the line with your left. Bring the rod up very slowly until the line arcs down behind you in a broad curve. Make sure the curve of the line is at least a foot behind you. When it is, push the rod forward and – at the end of the cast – downward. The line will roll like a hoop on the grass or pavement. (It will do likewise on the water when you actually start fishing with a floating line.)

Practice the roll cast many times. Observe that the leader and "fly" want to fall onto the line before they are fully extended. One way to prevent this mix-up is to pull the rod back slightly just before the line is fully extended.

Now you will learn to put together a roll cast with a back cast and forward cast. You will see this maneuver frequently at fly-fishing and outdoor shows. Though it may seem spectacular, you can learn to do it quite nicely in a short time.

Hold the rod in your right hand and the line in your left. Line is stretched out in front of you, and the rod points forward. Bring the line up slowly until it is well behind you, as in the roll cast. Roll the line out, and watch the leader and "fly" closely. Just before they hit the casting surface, pick the rod up smartly and make a back cast. Now pause, catch your breath, and bring the rod forward to complete the operation. Wasn't that nice?

During many of these elementary casting instructions, you must have noticed that the line wants to travel in the direction in which you propel it. This little phenomenon is the basis for "shooting" more line.

Earlier, I said, "The line will travel as far in front

In false casting, allow the line to get fully extended in front of you before you begin to bring the rod backward.

To learn the roll cast, start with the line stretched out ahead of you and then very slowly bring rod and line to this position.

One way to prevent the leader and fly from falling onto the fly line during a roll cast is to pull back a bit on the rod at finish.

In preparation for "shooting" line to lengthen your cast, pull three or four extra feet of line off reel and let it lie on casting surface.

of you as you have thrown it behind you." Now I want to elaborate on that statement and begin teaching you how to shoot extra line on your forward cast.

Prepare to make a simple overhead cast of 18 or 20 feet, as you already have done many times. Before you make the cast, however, pull three or four feet of extra line off the reel and let it lie on the casting surface. (If you were wading, the line would float on the water.)

With your left hand, grab the line up close to the rod's first guide. Bring the rod up with your right hand and at the same time move your left hand as far away from the rod as possible. Wait until the line is straight behind you, and then come forward into your cast also following the rod with your left hand. When you're sure the line is moving forward, release it from your left hand. The extra three or four feet lying on the ground should uncoil and fly up through the guides, adding welcome distance to your cast. Isn't that great?

You will learn advanced casting techniques in due time, depending on the kind and size of the water you choose to fish. For the moment, however, the simple overhead cast, the roll cast, and the little "shoot" will enable you to fly fish for trout or other kinds of fish in a large number of angling situations.

3

Fishing: 3 Hours

Fly fishing is divided into two major categories: wet fly and dry fly. The wet fly penetrates the surface of the water and sinks. The dry floats on the surface.

Wet flies are designed to enter the water quickly. They have a swept-back look. They may also be tied on heavier hooks, or sometimes tied with a lead or copper underlayment. They can be fished on a line designed to sink and help get the flies down in the water.

The dry fly is designed to float. It has an upright look. The hackles or feather on a dry fly are perpendicular to the hook shank. The hook and the rest of the fly are supported by the combined flotation of the individual tips of the hackle barbs. The dry fly may be

The traditional wet fly has wings and a swept-back look and is tied sparsely. The hackle feather is soft and comes from hens or gamebirds.

The typical dry fly has a stiff "at attention" look. Hackle feathers come from cock roosters and are stiff.

tied on a light hook. Generally the dry fly is fished on a floating line, which helps keep it on the surface.

The wet fly can imitate the water-bred and shore-bred insects, minnows, small fish, worms, and other creatures that like to inhabit the water. The dry fly can imitate many of the same creatures, but not all of them and not in all stages of the creature's life.

Both styles of fly fishing have advantages, and many anglers enjoy both. The wet fly is supposed to be easier, however, so let's begin with it.

Insect Imitations

Perhaps the broadest and most popular category of wet-fly fishing involves the imitation of insects, either those that are born and die in the water or those that are born near the water and get blown onto it or fall on it from other causes. No matter, the trout eat them all.

Streamborn insects go through certain stages over a varying period of time before they become airborne and leave the water. Life starts with an egg, then develops into a larva or nymph, the crawling, swimming, or flightless stage. Finally the insect becomes an adult fly whose sole purpose seems to be to start the cycle over again.

Fish will eat the streamborn insects in any stage they can find them. The easiest and most exciting time, however, is when the insect emerges into its adult stage. Until that moment, the insect has been reasonably hidden from the fish, in the stream bottom, under rocks, or in weeds. The insect's journey to the surface or to the bank is the most perilous time of its life.

When many insects of the same type or family emerge at the same time, you see what's known as a "hatch." The fish and the fisherman love a hatch. And you'll learn to love it, too, and watch and pray for it on the water you fish.

Wet Flies

Wet flies can be made and fished to imitate both the nymph and the adult stages of streamborn insects. In fact, it is difficult sometimes to say whether a trout has taken your fly because it resembled a nymph or an adult fly.

The nymph is a simpler form of insect. It has no wings, as does the adult fly. On some insects, the nymph's mouth and body parts are not fully developed. The imitation nymph consequently will look quite naked and unadorned when compared to the imitation adult wet fly or imitation adult dry fly.

But that's enough entomological theory. Let's go fishing with the wet fly. You're at the river's bank now with the same rod, reel, and floating line you used in learning to fly cast.

You have the same 9-foot leader, and you tie on a wet fly that has its hook barb pinched down. (Ideally, the choice of your first wet fly should be made by talking to people in local fly shops or other local fly fishermen. Barring that, try a Hare's Ear, Black Gnat, Cahill, Gordon, March Brown, or one of my soft-hackled flies.) Check the knot section of this book to learn how to tie the leader to your fly.

Our river is perhaps 50 or 60 feet wide. It has a nice flow, which you can feel against your waders (try to borrow a pair at this stage) as the water piles up against them on the upstream side. Our river has a series of riffles and pools, with some deep sides and some shallow sides.

You enter the river at the head of a riffle on the shallow side and pull 10 or 12 feet of line off the reel, shaking the rod tip as you did previously. You see immediately that the current will become an important part of fishing with the fly, because it is already taking the line, leader, and fly downstream.

Now you can pull another 8 or 10 feet of line off the reel and make your first cast across the stream to the deep side of the riffle. Hold the line in your left hand, as you did earlier, and follow the line down with the rod tip. Keep your eyes where you believe your fly is. It will make a quarter of a circle and will soon be trailing in the shallow water almost directly downstream from you. You have made your first wet cast.

Take a step downstream and cast again to the side of the stream. Follow the line and the slightly sunken fly as it moves in the current to a position below you.

At this stage in your fishing career, it's a good idea to keep the line taut between you and the fly. This way, you'll feel a trout when one rises to your fly.

When you feel the first one, it's not necessary to set the hook too hard into the fish. Just lift the rod slightly over your right hand and pull the line away from the rod with your left hand. You should learn from the start, in case you hook a big fish, to transfer the line immediately from your left hand to a spot between the forefinger of your right hand and the cork handle. This tactic will permit you to fight the fish directly off the reel, winding in when the fish tires, and letting the fish take line off the reel whenever it wants to.

Fighting a big trout, say one or two pounds or more, involves that kind of exchange. Right at the beginning of such a battle, you'll hold the rod high and let the fish tear line off the reel. You'll enjoy the sound. The trout will stop, and then it's your turn. You retrieve the line, and the trout resists. Then it runs again. When the fish stops, you retrieve line. And so the battle goes until the fish gets off or you have it tired at your feet.

You can land a smallish trout without a net. Just reel until the junction of your fly line and leader reaches the tip guide, turn yourself upstream, forming a loop in the rod, and reach down with your left hand to unhook the fly from the fish. Because you have previously pinched the barb down, the hook will

In fishing the wet fly, follow the line as it moves downstream and hold it in your left hand. Watch where you think fly is.

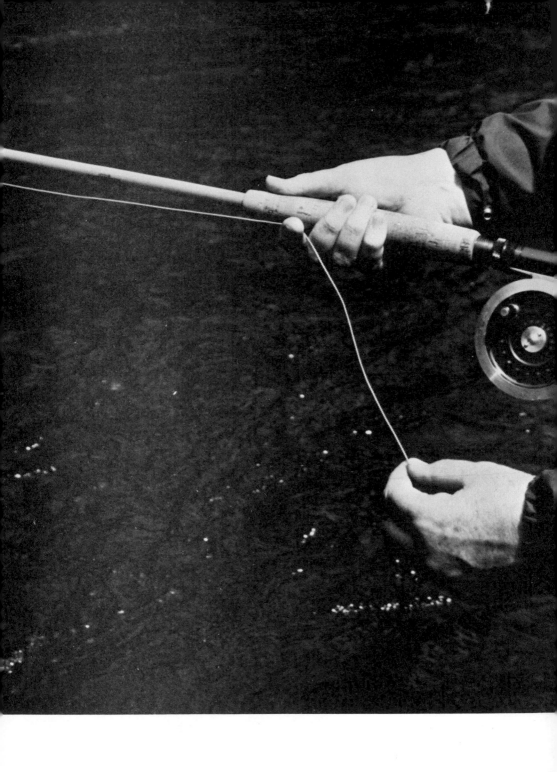

An invaluable trick of the trade: Before retrieving, transfer the line to spot between your right forefinger and cork grip.

come out quite easily. With this method, you avoid touching the fish at all, thereby practically guaranteeing its survival.

Sometimes you will fight a fish to exhaustion and it will seem lifeless. If this happens, spread your legs over the fish, bend down, and cup it gently in your hands, rightside up, holding its head upstream. The current will start to pass through the gills, which extract oxygen from the water, and the fish should recover. Balance it there until you can feel the life coming back, or until the fish can maintain itself in the current. Soon it will swim off. If there is not much current, move the fish slowly forward and back to get water flowing through its gills.

Should you be lucky enough to hook a steelhead or a trout or salmon of 5 pounds or more, you can still land it without a net, just by walking the fish up a gently sloping bank. Unhook it quickly and set it back in the water, rightside up.

When you're fly fishing, you usually don't need to jerk the fly in an attempt to entice a trout to take it. There are times, however, when the slightest movement, hesitation, or sideways motion of the fly will change a fish's mind.

This reaction can occur during a hatch. You can see the fish feeding. Throw the fly two or three feet upstream of the fish, and let it start to drift. When you think the fly is just in front of the fish, tighten the line slightly. Often you will see a boil or curl in the water that indicates the fish's interest in your fly. And you should feel the welcome tug.

When you're fishing down a riffle with the wet fly, you might want to try catching a fish after the line has straightened out completely below you. You can do this by holding the line against the rod handle with the forefinger of your right hand. With your left hand, pull the line in short steps through the forefinger. Between pulls, clamp the line firmly with the forefinger against the cork handle. This method, by the way, is the one by which you retrieve line in order to prepare for your next cast and later when you fish upstream with a nymph or dry fly.

Fly fishing of any kind demands only a little common sense and physical coordination. Nearly everyone qualifies. If, for instance, you see a half-inch brown insect on the water or flying about your head, tie on a brown imitation, approximately half an inch long, and throw it toward the fish. Chances are pretty good he'll take it.

Nymph Fishing

You could take any so-called nymph sold in any fly shop (or will tie yourself) and fish it quite successfully the way you did the wet fly. But you couldn't say you were nymph fishing. You would just be wet-fly fishing with a nymph pattern.

No, to fish with a nymph properly, you should

A recent development in fly fishing is fishing with nymphs such as this simple undressed pattern.

think about wading upstream and fishing up instead of down. This strategy will be a little more challenging than what you've done so far. You'll need to do more casting and more line manipulation. And initially, you will not catch as many fish.

As I said earlier, most of the nymph's life is spent hidden from the fish. The nymph becomes vulnerable at hatching time or if it happens to lose its hold on weed or rock.

When that happens, the nymph goes wherever the current takes it, without moving from one side to the other or from one depth to another. One of the best ways to imitate this phenomenon is to pitch the nymph upstream and let the current carry it down over and past the trout. This approach is called a "dead drift."

Retrieve your line and leader ahead of the fly at a speed equal to the speed of the current. If you pull the line too fast, you'll jerk the fly. If you pull the line too slow, you'll lose touch with the fly and be unable to set the hook when a fish rises.

Perhaps you are asking a question: "How do I know when a trout intercepts my fake nymph, particularly if I can't see it?" The answer is: "Stopping."

If you see the line stop (watch the line where it joins the leader), raise the rod tip and tighten on the line in your left hand. Incidentally, in this kind of fishing you have been pulling the line through the guides ahead of the fly in short steps beneath your right forefinger (which presses against the rod handle) and letting the extra line be swept downstream below you.

The most difficult part of upstream nymph fishing is to see the line stop or to sense in some intuitive way that a trout has taken your fly. You can use a strike indicator to help you see the stop. It's merely a piece of brightly colored yarn attached where the line joins the leader.

Dry Flies

What you have learned about nymph fishing will help prepare you for dry-fly fishing. You fish upstream. You pull the line down ahead of the fly so that it will seem to move naturally.

But dry-fly fishing involves differences.

One is that the dry fly must be waterproofed and then dried repeatedly in the air to make it float. (Perhaps you always wondered why the angler you saw in a trout river did this false casting over and over.)

The other big difference is that you can see the dry fly drift and see the trout take it. That aspect of dry-fly fishing makes it the most visible of all ways to fish a fly and—for many anglers—the most enchanting or rewarding way.

In the old days (when dry-fly fishing started in England in the middle or late part of the last century) the dry-fly fisherman would fish only the rise. That is, he wetted no line until he saw a trout rise to a natural insect. He tied on an artificial that imitated the real thing in size, shape, and color. Then he chucked it out to the fish, hoping to convince it that here was another tasty natural. Between hatches, the angler sat down, smoked a pipe, and contemplated the sport and life in general.

The idea of fishing only the rise has prevailed only little in North America. Most of us fish the "water" with a dry fly even though we see no hatch and no rising fish. We fish likely spots that may hold trout, and we try to tempt one to come up to the artificial. Another tactic is to try making the trout believe that a hatch is starting. You can also fish dry imitations of bees, horse flies, grasshoppers, beetles, ants, and a variety of other terrestrials (insects from the land). They come and go throughout the season and need no hatch to make them appealing to trout.

If you intend to fish with a dry fly, you must use a dry-fly floatant. Basically, it is a combination of wax and a fast-drying solvent. You dip the fly into the mixture or paint the solvent on with a brush. Let the fly dry, and it's ready.

Now for a little dry-fly fishing. Start wading upstream. There, 20 feet ahead and a little to your left, you see a trout rise. Take a couple of steps more upstream to get closer and be able to cast a shorter line.

You see the trout rise again, in the same spot. You pull 18 or 20 feet of line off the reel and start to false cast, alternately behind you and then ahead of you toward the feeding trout. (You practiced this earlier on dry land.) You're not only drying out the fly but you're also measuring the distance between you and where you saw the fish.

You cast, but the fly falls short. So you retrieve the line, pull another two feet off the reel, and start over. While you're false casting, the trout rises again, pinpointing the spot exactly for you.

You cast, and the fly lands two feet beyond (upstream of) the spot and starts to float down to the fish. The anticipation makes your heart pound. The trout rises to your fly. You want to set the hook now, but if you do you'll miss him. Delay just a second. Now tighten, and you've got him.

You fight this noble fish and release him carefully. You notice the fly is matted down, so you rinse it in the stream. Then, holding the leader an inch in front of the fly, you whisk it back and forth in the air to dry it out. Now you can dress the fly again with the floatant and fish again.

You have now learned the rudiments of dry-fly fishing over a rising trout. You can use the same system to fish the "water." A growing school of anglers fish the dry fly downstream with various casting techniques. The most popular of these is the "reach" cast. It's not easily explained to beginners, so you'll have to see it done and learn from what you see as you progress in your fly fishing.

Non-Insect Imitations

Streamers

Streamers represent non-insect creatures such as

*The streamer, of which this is a typical example, is the
most streamlined of flies. In the water, it most resembles
small prey fish.*

71

Among the many good spots in which you can fish a streamer effectively is the area under an overhanging tree.

small fish, crawfish, or frogs. The fishing technique is much like the one you use with the wet fly.

You throw the streamer as far as you can toward the far bank, pulling it in short or long draws across the stream as the line swings down below you. You make these draws by pulling line with your left hand through the forefinger of your right hand on the rod handle. After each pull you tighten the finger. In a good, strong current you can merely raise and lower the rod tip, letting the current do the work. Or you can fish the streamer without motion as with an ordinary wet fly.

Streamer fishing is a searching type of fly fishing. It also works well in periods of high or dirty water as well as in early spring before the insect hatches have come and in late fall after they have gone. You can be creative with the streamer, fishing it in ways that no other method can duplicate.

Now for a little streamer fishing in your stream. Notice the overhanging tree on the far bank. The lowest branches are perhaps three feet above the water, but you can see a nice deep pool there and an undercut bank. Most fly fishermen would pass up this place for fear of losing the fly in the tree.

If you can squeeze your streamer fly (Royal Coachman bucktail with barb pinched down, for example) between the branches and the water surface, you just might wake up what's sleeping in the hole or under the bank and be surprised with a very nice trout.

In situations like this, you want to fish as short a line as possible. The short line gives you accuracy and control. So you wade to within 10 or 12 feet of the most outstretched branches if you can safely do so. You won't cast overhead. Instead, you'll hold the rod almost parallel to the river and throw the fly under the tree about the way a baseball pitcher might deliver a sidearm curve over the plate.

You make the first cast and miss the tree. The Royal Coachman bucktail falls just short of where you want it. You fish the fly through anyway, and you can see it working two or three inches below the surface in the dark water.

You've got to lengthen your cast three feet. So you retrieve the line and pull three feet of line off the reel. Then you start sidearm casting again. And pitch. This time the fly just avoids the low-hanging branches and drives deep under them, close to the bank.

The streamer sits still for a second, and you give it a jerk. Bang! What was that? Where did that fish come from? He's on. A little creativity and your willingness to gamble a fly in a hazardous spot have paid off.

That's streamer fishing. Some anglers swear by it and have never learned to fish the dry fly or the ordinary wet fly. It's a good idea to carry a couple of streamer patterns around with you and try them whenever the mood hits you. A good time to fish streamers is from dawn until the sun's rays hit the water. Another good time is the hour before total darkness and (where it's legal) an hour after.

Adapting to Still Water

You can take your fly rod and fish any of the four types of flies I've mentioned (wet, nymph, dry, or streamer) on any lake or farm pond and be very successful. The one thing you'll lack, though, is the current. So you must do for yourself the work the current normally does for you in a stream. You can still throw a dry fly and let it sit motionless until a fish rises to it. You can cast a wet fly and let it sink to the desired depth and retrieve it slowly at the speed necessary to attract the fish. The same goes for a nymph or streamer. Without the current, you might need to be a little more positive in setting the hook. That's probably the major difference.

4

Knots: 1 Hour

Backing to Reel

Don't let this part scare you. You've already got a good grasp of fly fishing's hard parts.

The basic knots you need in fly fishing are quite simple. First you must attach the fly line to the reel. By itself, a regular fly line of 30 yards usually will not fill up your reel's space. Besides, when you get into a big strong fish, you will need a line much longer than 30 yards. The solution? Put backing on the reel first.

Backing is a strong braided line of fairly small diameter. The good fly-shop owner or clerk will advise you on how many yards you need. He may also offer to do this work, including attaching the fly line and leader for you, if you've bought your outfit from him.

A simple way to attach backing to your reel: Start by passing tag end of backing through line guard, around reel arbor (spool), and back out through line guard. Next, tie a simple overhand knot close to line's end and pull it fairly snug. Then, as shown, tie a second overhand knot, this one encircling the standing (main) part of the line. Then pull slowly on the standing part of the line until the knots slide together and jam against the reel arbor.

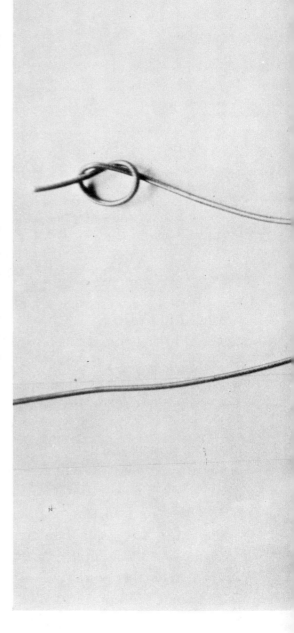

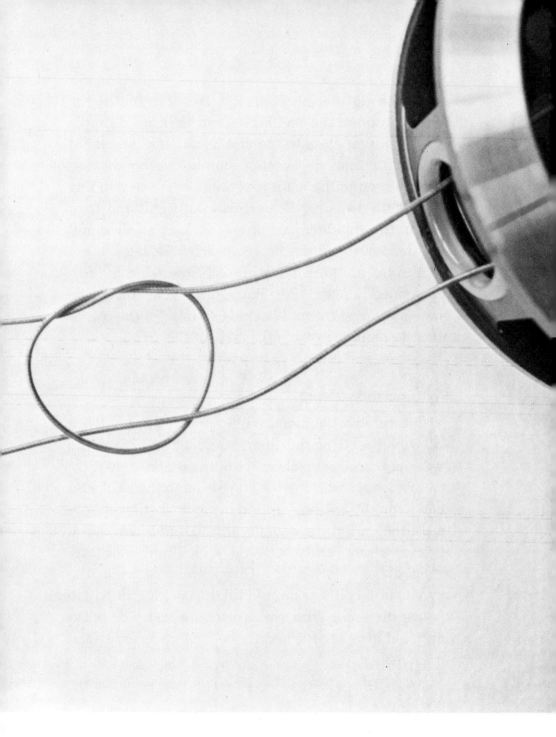

If you do the job yourself, pass the end of the backing around the reel arbor, and then tie a simple overhand knot close to the end. Now take the end of the backing and tie another simple overhand knot, this one around the main part (known as the standing part) of the backing. Draw this knot tight, and then pull on the standing part of the backing to slide and jam the knot against the reel's arbor. (Check these steps in the accompanying photo.) Now wind the recommended length of backing onto your reel. The combination of line and backing should fill the reel to about ⅛ of an inch from the edge of the spool.

Fly Line to Backing

Information included with most fly lines will tell you which end of the line should be joined to the backing. Uncoil several inches of the fly line and form it into a loop. Insert the backing through the loop, and then wrap the backing around the loop six times. Now insert the end of the backing through the loop, holding everything firmly between your thumb and forefinger of your left hand. (Check these steps in the accompanying illustration.) Pull the backing slowly to tighten the knot. Trim any protruding end. The backing could also be attached to the fly line as explained in the next step.

Leader Butt to Fly Line

As soon as you have wound your fly line onto the

reel, you should tie a stout piece of nylon leader material to the end of the line. The nylon should be at least a foot long and about two-thirds the diameter of the fly line's end. For a 6-weight line, this diameter would be about 20 or 25 thousandths of an inch (.020" to .025") and a breaking strain of 20 or 25 pounds. This is a permanent part of the fly line and can be tied by following the steps in the accompanying illustration. (For learning any of these knots, use thicker material such as clothesline for practice till you get the hang of things.)

Here's how to join fly line to backing with the Albright Knot. Unwind a foot or so of fly line from its plastic spool. Form a loop in the end of the fly line. Insert the tag end of the backing through the loop from the rear, and then wrap 6 turns of backing around the loop from left to right. Tuck the tag end of the backing through the front of the loop. Hold coils securely between your left thumb and forefinger. Slowly pull on the standing part of the backing until the coils snug up into a tight, even knot. Trim tag ends. — Drawing courtesy of Scientific Anglers/3M.

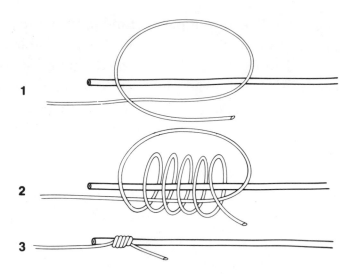

Follow these steps to tie leader butt to fly line: 1. Hold line tip over leader butt. Form a loop in the leader in front of the line. 2. Pass the leader end through the loop and over the line 5 or 6 times. 3. Pull on the leader end to snug up the wraps evenly and tighten the knot. Trim tag ends. Dab ends with cement to smooth joint and improve its sliding through rod guides. —Drawing courtesy of Scientific Anglers/3M.

Leader Section to Leader Section

The leader, with all of its sections tied together, should be at least 9 feet long. Sometimes a leader is as long as 18 or 20 feet, depending on the kind of fishing you do. The leader is tapered (each section of smaller diameter than the previous one) to permit a finer pre-

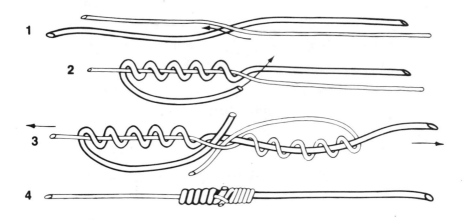

For joining one section of the leader to another, follow these step-by-step instructions to tie a Blood Knot, sometimes called a Barrel Knot. This example illustrates tying tippet (final section) to leader. 1. Lay one end of the tippet over the leader end to form an X. Allow about 4 to 6 inches of each to tie knot. 2. Hold the X between your right thumb and forefinger. Using your left hand, make 5 turns of the leader end around the tippet, wrapping away from you. Bring the leader end back and insert it on the other side of the X. At this point, switch the knot to hold it between your left thumb and forefinger. 3. Using your right hand, make five turns of the tippet around the leader, wrapping toward you. Bring the tippet end back and insert it into the same opening that the leader end is in, but in the opposite direction. Now wet the wraps with saliva and tighten the knot by pulling steadily on the two standing ends. 4. To finish the knot, trim the two tag ends. — Drawing courtesy of Scientific Anglers/3M.

sentation to the fish and to aid in the mechanics of casting. The breaking strain of the leader depends on the strength of the tippet, the final and thinnest section of the leader. The fly is attached to the tippet.

In the normal course of fishing several hours, you will change the fly many times, lose a fly now and then in a tree, and perhaps lose a fly in a fish's mouth.

When you change flies, you shorten the leader. If you took no remedial action, you'd eventually work

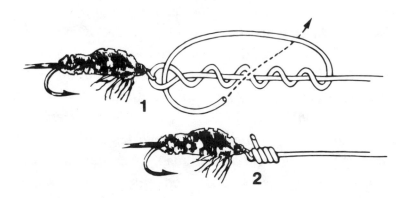

Here's how to tie the Improved Clinch Knot: 1. Thread tippet through the hook eye, and pull out about 6 inches. Make 5 turns with tag end of the tippet around the standing part. Push end through the loop created in front of the hook eye—and then bring the end back through the big loop just formed. 2. Wet the knot and pull steadily on the tippet to tighten the twists against the hook eye. Trim tag end. —Drawing courtesy of Scientific Anglers/3M.

your way back to a heavier section than the tippet you started out with.

To maintain the tippet's original length and diameter, you must occasionally add some new material to the tippet. Use a Blood Knot, or Barrel Knot. It's the same knot you use to join the leader's first section to the butt section, which is attached to the fly line. The progressively thinner sections of the leader are joined in the same way.

The blood knot may look simple in the drawings, but it requires some practice.

Use the same number of turns on one side of the monofilament as on the other. Poke the ends of the material through the space in the center of the knot, and then pull sections of material until the knot tightens. Trim the ends close with your clippers.

For details on how to tie this knot, see the accompanying drawing and caption.

Fly to Tippet

The most commonly used knot to join the fly to the leader tippet today is the Improved Clinch Knot. Learn how to tie it by following the steps in the accompanying drawings and caption.

5

Fly Tying:
1 Hour

Trout flies, if you buy them, are expensive, averaging at least a dollar for wet or dry patterns, nymphs, and streamers. You can make flies yourself for a lot less. In fact, the cost of tying your own flies is only a little more than the cost of the hook, which will be about 5 or 6 cents. Some dry flies, requiring fine rooster hackles, could cost twice that much.

But you don't tie flies to save money. You tie them because it's fun. Most of the materials are enjoyable to look at and work with. You can tie in the dead of winter when there's no fly fishing. And you get a special pleasure in catching and releasing trout or other fish on the flies you tied yourself.

You can tie a few simple flies, without spending a great deal of money, by following the instructions I'll give you. If you like the activity, you can buy more-sophisticated equipment and supplies from your local fly-fishing dealer. He probably will also offer fly-tying classes. Another source of lessons is your local chapter of Trout Unlimited or Federation of Fly Fishers. Some colleges and adult-education curriculums also offer fly-tying classes.

In this book's "crash" course in fly fishing, you'll learn by doing to tie a streamer, wet fly, and dry fly. You'll use simple equipment and materials, most of which you can find in your own home.

You'll need some sort of vise to hold the hook. A regular handyman's vise will do. Or a pair of square-nosed pliers. Or some sort of clamp. Or a pair of hemostats.

I started tying flies many years ago with the help of a pair of square-nosed pliers. Just insert the round bend of the hook into the jaws and wrap a strong rubber band around the handles, to provide tension. Set the pliers into the corner of a shallow cardboard box or on the corner of a table and weighted with a book to hold them steady. You can do the same thing with a pair of hemostats if they're strong enough to hold the hook.

You'll also need a pair of scissors and a spring-loaded clothespin. Tweezers will come in handy, too. Some thin, strong thread. And the following materials:

- Feathers of any sort, but preferably at least two or three inches long (try a pillow).

- Some yarn or wool.
- And hair from a dog, cat, squirrel, goat, or any other animal. (Or try an old fur coat.)

Fly tying is a very apt expression to describe what you'll be doing. Thin, strong thread ties in the material. The thread advances up the hook ahead of the material. The material follows the thread and is then tied off. Feathers and fur are tied in by thread. They can be wrapped around the hook or laid flat and tied off again by thread. The final wrapping of thread is at the head of the fly, where you'll use half-hitch knots to secure the thread. If you're not too certain about the knot, you can cement the head with clear nail polish.

Streamer Fly

Mount the hook in the vise or pliers. (I have used my own professional vise in the photos.) Start the thin, strong thread at the tail of the hook. Hold the end in your left hand and the rest in your right. Form an oblique angle from left to right, and wind the thread over itself. Now grab the thread with a clothespin and let it hang. Trim the excess first end with your scissors.

Tie in a piece of brightly colored wool or yarn that's three or four inches long. Wind the thread ahead to within ⅛-inch of the hook eye, and let the thread hang again with the clothespin. Wrap the wool around the hook in a neat and even layer until you catch up to the thread. Tie the thread around the wool

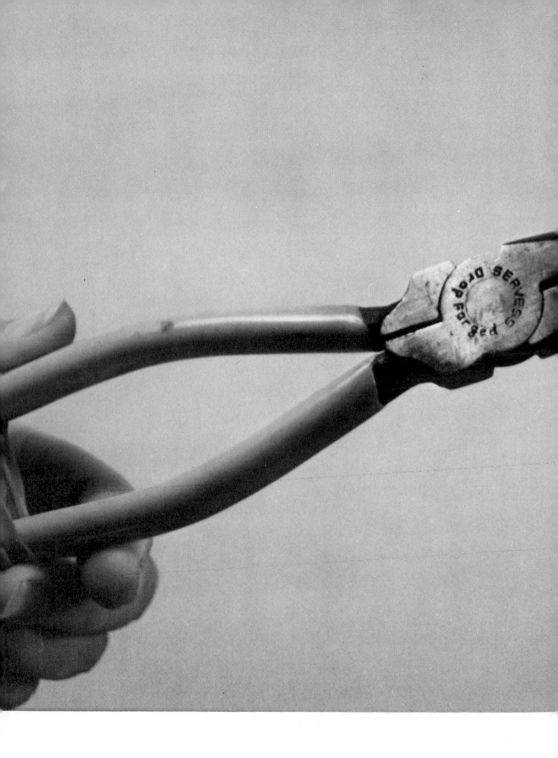

90

For your first fly-tying projects, you can make a vise, as I did decades ago, from square-nosed pliers with a strong rubber band wrapped around the handles.

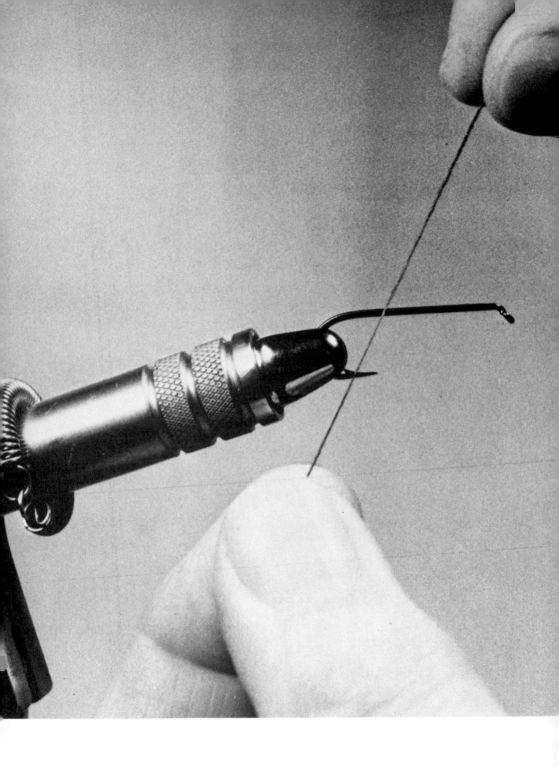

The key to attaching the tying thread is to start it at an angle like this. Second turn goes over the first and binds it.

When the tying thread is firmly secured, you can hang a spring-loaded clothespin on the loose end to keep everything taut while you get material for next step.

Tie in end of the body material at rear of hook, and then advance the tying thread in windings as shown toward hook eye. Again let clothespin hang on tying thread to hold things taut.

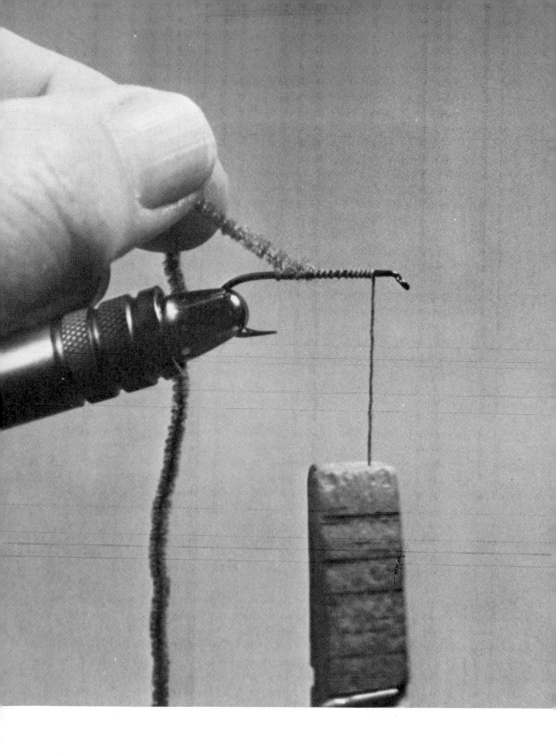

Wrap the body material around the hook in neat and even turns until you catch up to the tying thread. Tie thread around the material and trim excess.

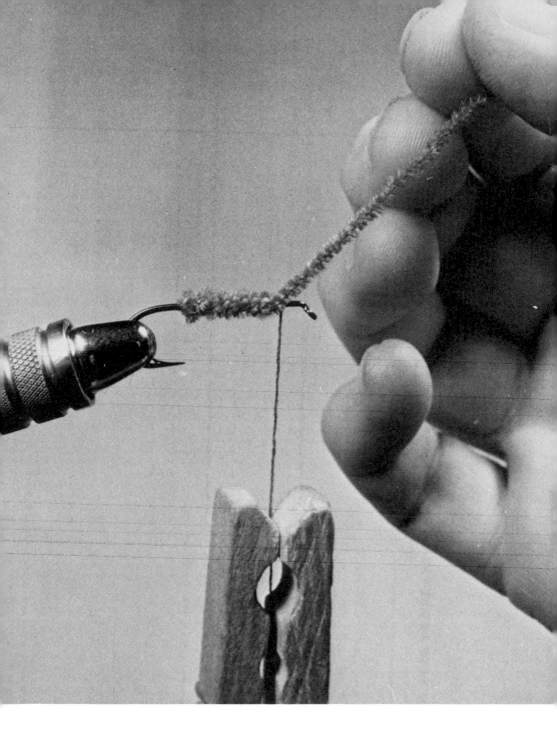

in front of it and behind it. Cut off the excess wool close to the hook.

Before tying the wing on in the next step, you can put a drop of clear nail polish on the windings to hold the wing.

Now take some longish hair from a dog, cat, or other handy animal. Keep the hair ends even, and hold the bunch tightly between the thumb and forefinger of your right hand at the front of the hook to "measure" the right length. The tips of the hair should not extend too far past the bend of the hook.

Now, pass the hairs in a bunch to your left hand. Hold them over the head of the hook, but not on it. Now bring the thread up between the hair and your thumb, raising your thumb just enough to catch the thread. Make a loop over the top of the hair, bring the thread back down on the other side, catching it this time between the hair and your forefinger. Now pull downward on the thread, bringing the bunch of hairs with it on top of the hook.

Between your fingers, you will feel the thread tighten over the clump of hairs. Do not release your fingers from the hairs. Keep them tight. Do three or four more turns with the thread before releasing your fingers. Now, the bunch of hairs should sit on top of the hook. Cut off the excess that hangs over the eye of the hook. (Many other materials in fly tying are tied similarly on top of the hook.) The material usually tends to follow the thread to the other side of the hook. The method I've just explained helps keep the material on top.

Now wrap the thread neatly toward the eye of the hook, aiming to create a taper. You finish the fly with a series of half-hitches. To tie a half-hitch, start by pulling the thread taut with your left hand. Then pull on the thread with your right hand. Relax the pull, and let the thread twist itself into a loop. Place the loop over the head of the fly, and then pull the thread tight. Make several half-hitches before cutting off the excess thread.

What you have produced can be a very effective streamer fly. If you cannot get hair of any kind, you could use a couple of feathers tied on or another piece of wool with the ends frayed to represent the wing. Colors of materials can be varied. Silver or gold tinsel can also be spiraled around the body to give it sparkle. And other materials can be used to change patterns.

Wet Fly

Tie the thread onto the *front* of the hook. Wrap the thread in even layers toward the bend of the hook. Stop above the point of the hook, and then bring the thread back to the starting point in four even spirals. (For a fatter body, use wool or yarn, as in the streamer fly.) Take a feather (as soft a specimen as you can find), and remove the soft, furry barbs from the base of it. Then tie the feather's butt onto the hook. Trim

You can "measure" the length of wing material by holding the hair over the eye of the hook.

Hold the clump of wing hairs as shown, and bring the tying thread up and over several times before you release hold.

Here's how the streamer fly looks before you trim off the excess wing material at the eye of the hook.

I'm indebted to Charlie Vanerka for showing me how to tie a half-hitch this way. Make several behind hook eye before trimming thread.

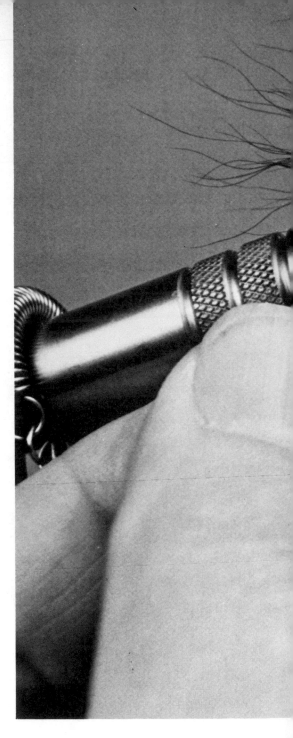

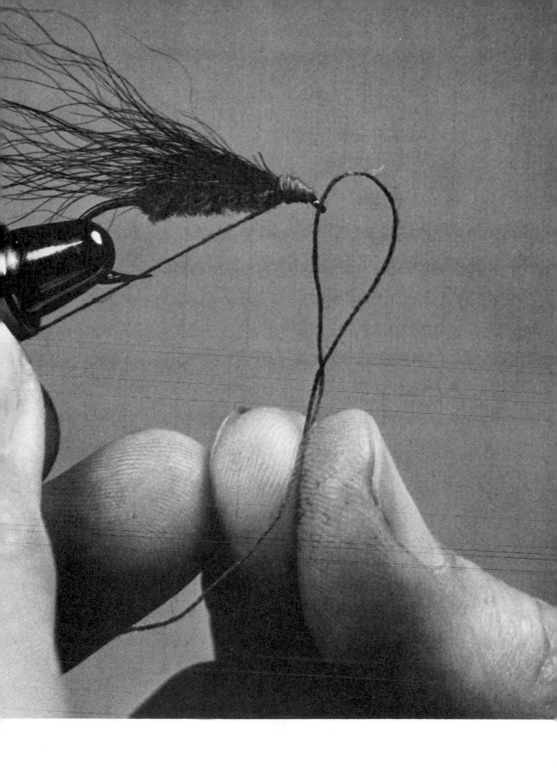

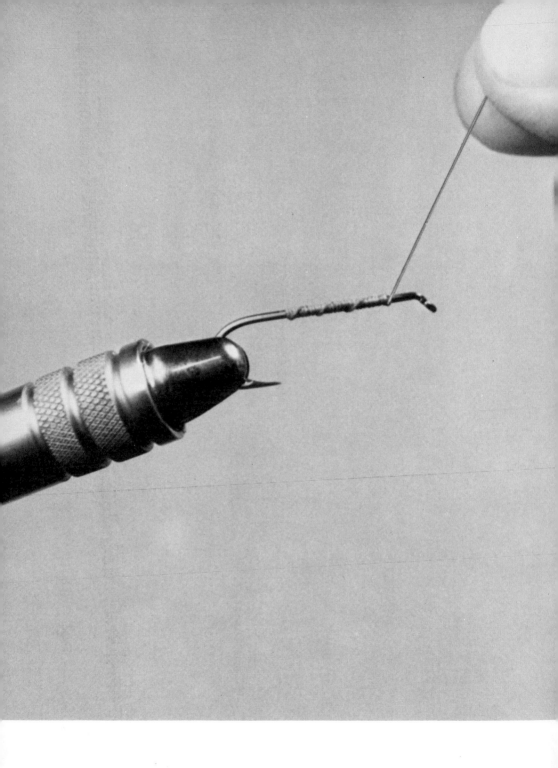

In tying a wet fly, start by tying thread onto front of hook. Wind thread back toward hook bend in tight, even turns; then come forward, as shown, in four even spirals.

Take the softest feather you can find in about this size, and tie its butt in near the eye of the hook.

While you trim feather's butt close to hook eye, tying thread is held taut by the hanging clothespin, out of photo.

Here's how the sparse wet fly looks after you wind the feather twice around the shank of hook, bind feather in place slanting backward with tying thread, apply finishing half-hitches, and trim thread.

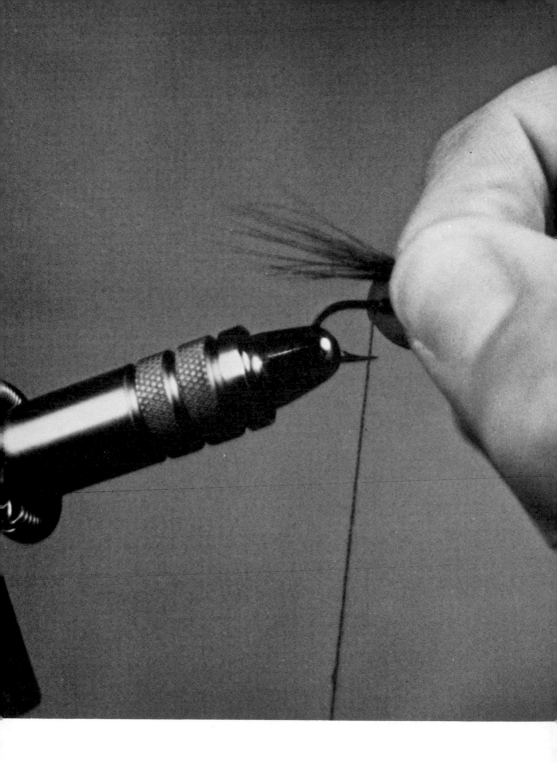

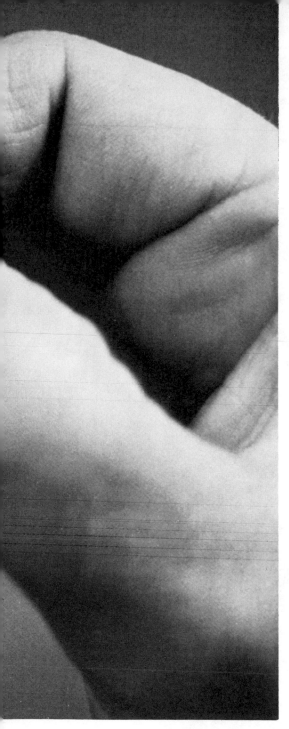

Typical dry fly has a tail, tied in above the hook's point. Tail helps the fly to float.

This close-up of finished dry fly shows what makes it float: The individual points of the hackle feathers that radiate straight out from the hook, and the points of the tail.

the excess butt. Grab the feather by the tip, and wrap it twice around the shank of the hook. Tweezers are a help in grabbing the tip of the feather.

Bring the thread up and wind it through the feather, in front of it, and behind it to hold it. Bind the feather down with your thumb and forefinger so that it slants backward. Trim. Finish in front of the feather and the head, and apply half-hitches as you did with the streamer.

Dry Fly

Use the same procedure you did for the wet fly. Stop the thread above the point of the hook. Tie in five or six barbs of a feather (preferably as stiff as you can find) in the same manner as tying in the streamer wing. Trim the ends. Then take the thread back to the head of the fly.

Take a long, stiff feather. Strip away and discard the soft, furry barbs from the base of it and tie the feather by the butt ⅛-inch behind the hook's eye. Cut the excess. Grab the feather by the tip with your fingers or with tweezers and wrap it as many times as you can around the hook's shank, moving *forward* with the feather as you wind it. Bring up the thread, and wrap it through and around the feather as you did with the wet fly. Try not to bind down any of the barbs. Let them stick out perpendicular to the hook shank. Trim. And finish the head with the half-hitches.

Index